INSIDE RECOVERY:

HOW THE TWELVE STEP PROGRAM CAN WORK FOR YOU

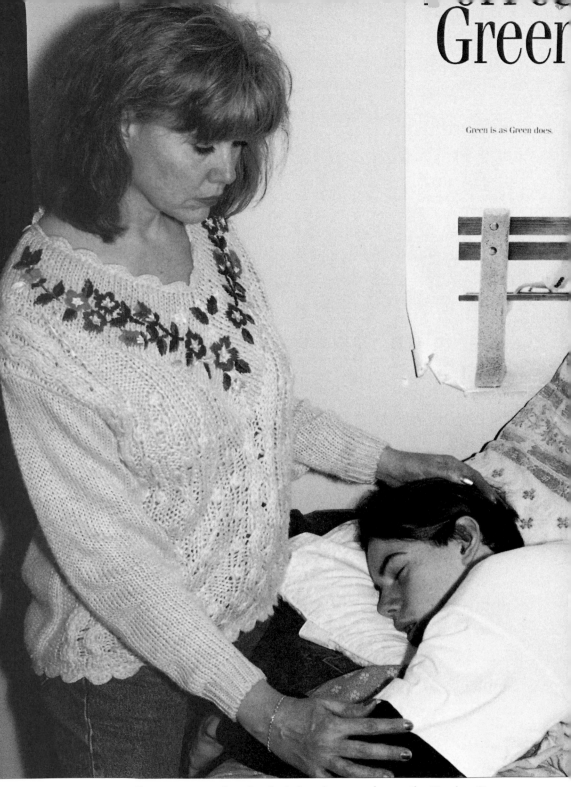

For many people who feel they have no hope, the Twelve Step Program can provide a successful path toward recovery.

INSIDE RECOVERY: HOW THE TWELVE STEP PROGRAM CAN WORK FOR YOU

Susan Banfield

THE ROSEN PUBLISHING GROUP, INC.
NEW YORK

To K. R. G.

The people pictured in this book are only models. They in no way practice or endorse the activities illustrated. Captions serve only to explain the subjects of photographs and do not in any way imply a connection between the real-life models and the staged situations.

Published in 1998 by The Rosen Publishing Group, Inc.
29 East 21st Street, New York, NY 10010

First Edition

Library of Congress Cataloging-in-Publication Data

Banfield, Susan.
    Inside Recovery: how the twelve step program can work for you / Susan Banfield.
    p. cm. -- (The drug abuse prevention library)
    Includes bibliographical references and index.
    Summary: Describes the practices and principles of twelve-step programs, how they can be used in dealing with such problems as alcoholism and drug addiction, and how to get involved in them.
    ISBN 0-8239-2634-6
    1. Teenagers—Alcohol use—United States—Juvenile literature.
2. Teenagers—Drug use—United States—Juvenile literature.
3. Twelve step programs—United States—Juvenile literature.
4. Alcoholics—Rehabilitation—United States—Juvenile literature.
5. Narcotic addicts—Rehabilitation—United States—Juvenile literature.
    [1. Twelve-step programs. 2. Alcoholism. 3. Drug abuse.] I. Title. II. Series.
HV5135.B355 1998
616.86′06—dc21   98-11797
                                         CIP
                                           AC

Manufactured in the United States of America

Contents

Introduction

Tim had been drinking ever since junior high. At first he drank because that's what the cool kids were doing. In the beginning he liked getting drunk with his friends. It made him feel brave and important.

Later Tim moved on to drinking almost every day. In the morning before leaving for school he would sneak whiskey from the bottle in his parents' liquor cabinet and replace it with water. He kept a bottle in his locker. In the evenings he would persuade one of the older boys on his street to get him a few beers.

Tim's cousin Joe, who was twenty-five, had tried to talk to Tim about his drinking. Tim knew that Joe had had a bad drinking problem when he was a teen, but that he had managed somehow to quit several years ago.

But Tim wasn't interested in what his cousin
*had to say. He liked being in with the fast
crowd, and he didn't see why people made
such a big deal about his drinking.*

*Most of the time now Tim drank by
himself. He had lost two after-school jobs
because he had gotten drunk and failed to
show up for work.*

*Most of Tim's friends were talking about
what they would do after they graduated in
June. Tim's grades had fallen off so much
that he couldn't really think about college.
His parents didn't seem to care, or notice how
much Tim was drinking.*

*Even the one bright spot in Tim's life
was fading fast. His steady girlfriend Meg
was threatening to leave him if he didn't
sober up and straighten out. They fought all
the time these days. Sometimes, when he was
drunk, Tim said things to her that he later
regretted. He felt as if he couldn't help
himself.*

*Tim had tried to quit drinking. He had
promised Meg several times he would stop.
But none of his resolutions had lasted longer
than a week. Somehow each time he found
himself with a beer in his hand. Then, once
he had the first one, he figured he'd already
blown it so he might as well get good and
drunk.*

8

One night early in his senior year Tim borrowed a friend's old Cadillac to take Meg out dancing. Luckily, Meg had refused to ride home with him. On the way back he got confused about the turnoff and drove the car straight into a telephone pole. When Tim woke up in the hospital he knew he had to talk to his cousin Joe.

Joe came down to the hospital that evening and talked to Tim for a long time. Joe described how it had finally hit him that, because of his drinking, he had ruined everything in life that mattered to him. He had realized that he couldn't stop, no matter how hard he tried. Then Joe described a program consisting of twelve steps that had helped him to get sober for good.

Tim realized that he was in the same place his cousin had been a few years back. And if Joe could get sober, maybe he could too.

Before he left that evening, Joe gave Tim a book that described the illness of alcoholism and explained how to recover by "working" the Steps. He called it the "Big Book" and told Joe to read it as soon as he was well enough.

Once Tim was out of the hospital, Joe introduced Tim to his friends in the fellowship called Alcoholics Anonymous. All of these

young men and women had once had serious |
drinking problems. Now they were keeping
sober and were eager to help Tim on the road
to recovery as well.

People who have an alcohol problem often sink to a point of utter despair—a "bottom"—much as Tim did. In the past, without treatment, many men and women who reached that point took their own lives, went insane, or were permanently locked up. Alcoholism was an affliction from which there was no known way out. But about sixty years ago, the founders of Alcoholics Anonymous developed a program to change that course.

In this book you will find out about the basic principles of the Twelve Step Program. It was first developed as a program to treat alcoholism, but since then Twelve Step groups have been formed for people who have other kinds of problems such as drug abuse, gambling, eating disorders, and codependency. If you or someone you know is suffering from one of these problems, you will learn more about how to stop its destructive course.

For many people who feel they have no hope, the Twelve Step Program can provide a successful path toward recovery.

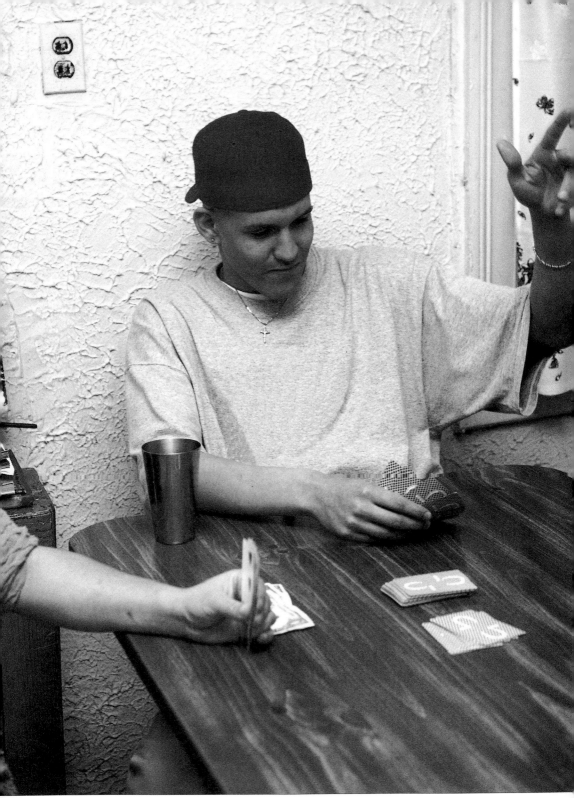

For many teens, gambling is more than just a game.

CHAPTER 1

What Is the Twelve Step Program?

*T*he Twelve Step Program is a program of recovery to help people with obsessive-compulsive problems.

An obsessive-compulsive problem is one in which someone has powerful, recurring thoughts (an "obsession") that force an action (a "compulsion"). Alcoholism is an example of an obsessive-compulsive pattern: an alcoholic drinks because he has recurring, unwanted thoughts of drinking so strong that they drive him to pick up a drink.

This pattern can be seen in other common problems, too. A compulsive gambler is driven to place a bet by obsessive thoughts about how this time he might win big. The compulsive eater is driven to

12 | binge by obsessive thoughts about food. The anorexic has obsessive thoughts about her weight and her body that compel her to starve herself. And a drug abuser may have obsessive thoughts about that next high that compel him to use drugs.

Anyone whose life is dominated by one of these, or any other obsessive-compulsive pattern, has a number of common emotions and behaviors. One of them is denial, or being unable to admit that you have a problem. You can't see how your behavior is harmful to yourself, and is becoming out of control.

Rationalization is also common. That means thinking up explanations that justify your behavior, or make it seem less dangerous than it really is. You make excuses such as "Everyone gets high on the weekends," "I only gamble on small games," or "I only stole a few things."

You also may become isolated, withdrawing from family and friends or driving them away with angry outbursts. You drink, take drugs, eat, or gamble alone. You are caught up in trying to make things go the way you want, and turn your back on things of a spiritual nature.

Tim, whose story you read in the introduction, is in many ways a typical alcoholic. Although his drinking may have

During the recovery period, it is common for people to feel remorse for having hurt their loved ones.

begun innocently, it soon became dangerous and out of control. One danger sign was when he began to drink by himself, not just when he was out with his friends. Also, Tim found it hard to stop once he started.

History of the Twelve Step Program

The Twelve Step Program began about sixty years ago with a quick-witted and ambitious New York stockbroker named Bill W. (In many Twelve Step groups, in order to protect anonymity, last names are not used.)

Bill W. had a long history of alcohol abuse. He had been unable to complete law school because he was too drunk to take his final exams, and he had lost many jobs because of his drinking.

13

14 Bill had become almost completely isolated—friends no longer wanted to have him around. And, much like Tim, he had nearly destroyed the one relationship left in his life—his marriage. He mistreated his wife when drunk, regretted it intensely when he dried out, made solemn promises to quit drinking, and then began the cycle all over again.

One bleak November, Bill sat at home drinking while his wife was at work. An old school friend, Ebby T., called and asked if he could stop by. Bill and Ebby had been drinking buddies for years. But from the sound of Ebby's voice, it was clear that today he was sober!

Bill was even more amazed when they met. He offered Ebby some of the pineapple juice and gin concoction he was drinking, and Ebby refused it. Bill couldn't resist asking him what this was all about.

Quietly Ebby explained how two months earlier he had become involved in a simple program of spiritual action. He told Bill how he applied the principles of the program: becoming honest about himself and his shortcomings, making amends for the harm he had done while drinking, practicing giving without thought of reward, and praying to God for guidance and help. The result, he said, was that he had been released from the desire to drink. He had been sober for two months now.

Bill could see plainly that, whatever Ebby had been doing, it was working. He had never seen his friend looking so clear-eyed and glowing. But Bill had trouble with the idea of God—at least with the idea of a personal God to pray to and receive guidance from. Bill wanted what his friend had achieved, but he could not bring himself to accept the ideas that Ebby was suggesting to him.

For days Bill fought within himself, turning over and over what Ebby had said. All the while he continued to drink. Then, in early December, he checked himself into the hospital one more time to dry out. As the effects of the alcohol wore off, Bill fell into a deep depression, full of remorse about the way he had treated his wife and utterly hopeless about the future.

Then, in the middle of his despair, Bill made the decision that turned his life around. Ebby had suggested to him that he might choose his own conception of God. Bill finally felt able to accept this and admit that he had a problem. He resolved—to God and to himself—that he would do anything in order to get well.

The first step in the recovery program is the need to admit defeat. Only then does a person realize the truth about his or her situation.

This decision changed everything. Bill felt profoundly peaceful. And he never took another drink.

It wasn't easy, though. One weekend Bill found himself alone in a strange city on business, and he felt the temptation to drink. He was frightened. The thought came to him, "You need another alcoholic to talk to." Bill called a clergyman from the hotel's church directory and asked if he knew of any drunks he could speak with. Soon he had a meeting arranged with a local physician, Dr. Bob.

The pattern of Dr. Bob's alcoholism was all too typical. He had been thrown out of one medical school and almost failed to get his degree. He was hanging on to his practice by the skin of his teeth; when he was drunk, he avoided going to the hospital or receiving patients.

Like Bill, Bob and his wife had been shunned by their friends. Also like Bill, Bob made repeated promises to his wife—which he couldn't keep—that he would quit drinking.

But all of this changed when Bob and Bill sat down to talk. Bob heard, from someone who understood alcoholism from actual experience, that it was possible to recover. Bill was not talking down to him from some spiritual hilltop. And something began to

18 | change inside Dr. Bob. Not long afterward, he had his last drink.

As a result of their experiences, Bill and Bob got together with other early recovered alcoholics and came up with the main elements of a program to save an alcoholic from a certain death. They included:

- admitting that you're licked, that you're powerless over alcohol
- making an inventory of your character flaws
- sharing your shortcomings with another person in confidence
- making amends to everyone you harmed while drinking
- trying to help other alcoholics with no thought of reward
- praying to whatever God you believe in for the power to do all these things

Within two years, using this approach, Bob and Bill managed to help about forty alcoholics get sober.

As time passed, Bill and Bob began to worry that their word-of-mouth approach was going too slowly and vast numbers of alcoholics would never hear the message of recovery. They also began to fear that as the program was passed from one alcoholic to another, its principles might be confused and changed. So they decided to write a book explaining in detail how to follow the program of recovery.

The "Big Book"

As the book was being written, the six points listed above were expanded into the Twelve Steps. They remain unchanged to this day.

Bill considered the breakdown into twelve steps necessary in order to be absolutely sure that anyone reading them would be left with no questions as to what he or she must do.

When *Alcoholics Anonymous*, affectionately called the "Big Book," was published in April 1939, the Twelve Steps appeared as follows:

1. We admitted we were powerless over alcohol—that our lives had become unmanageable.

2. Came to believe that a Power greater than ourselves could restore us to sanity.

3. Made a decision to turn our will and our lives over to the care of God <u>as we understood Him</u>.

4. Made a searching and fearless moral inventory of ourselves.

5. Admitted to God, to ourselves, and to another human being the exact nature of our wrongs.

6. Were entirely ready to have God remove all these defects of character.

7. Humbly asked Him to remove our shortcomings.

8. Made a list of all persons we had harmed, and became willing to make amends to them all.

9. Made direct amends to such people wherever possible, except when to do so would injure them or others.

10. Continued to take personal inventory and when we were wrong promptly admitted it.

11. Sought through prayer and meditation to improve our conscious contact with God as we understood Him, praying only for knowledge of His will for us and the power to carry that out.

12. Having had a spiritual awakening as the result of these steps, we tried to carry this message to alcoholics and to practice these principles in all our affairs.

By the end of 1939, membership in the Alcoholics Anonymous fellowship (named after the book) had shot up to 800. In 1941 a feature article in the *Saturday Evening Post* gave the organization further publicity, and by the end of that year there were more than 8,000 A. A. members. Throughout the 1940s and 1950s, A.A. continued to grow. Before long there were meetings in dozens of foreign countries.

Today—more than sixty years after it got its start—A.A. is helping millions of people all over the world. What's more, people with a wide variety of problems are finding recovery through the Twelve Steps.

CHAPTER 2

Problems Helped by the Twelve Steps

The Twelve Steps were originally intended as a program of recovery for alcoholics. But even the early members of A.A. recognized that the Steps laid out a way of life that could benefit anyone.

Eventually, as you read in chapter 1, people found that the Steps also helped other problems in the same dramatic way they helped alcoholism.

Compulsive Gambling

Gerry was known at school as Kingpin. Ever since he could remember, Gerry had loved to go down to the local arcade and play the pinball machines. The machines gobbled up most of Gerry's weekly allowances and the money he made from his paper route. Even now he often spent Saturday nights there, no matter what the rest of his friends were doing. He blew much of the weekly paycheck he received from his part-time job.

Gerry also loved playing cards. Every Wednesday night his uncles and aunts gathered at his house for a weekly poker game. As soon as his mother and father let him, Gerry began joining in. By high school, he played not only Wednesday nights with his family (where you could never win much), but whenever he could join a game in the neighborhood or could get one together among his friends.

And then there were Gerry's bets on foot-ball games. In high school, he got to know a group of older boys who sold what they called "football tickets." These weren't really tickets, but betting sheets for college and pro games. He thought nothing about spending twenty or thirty dollars on one of these tickets.

Gerry justified his card games and his sports betting to himself, saying he was dreaming of the day when he would win big and be able to buy a car or a motorcycle and impress all his friends. He also wanted to buy his mother the fur coat she had wanted for so long.

But the truth was, Gerry hardly had enough money to go out for hamburgers after

24 | *school. As soon as he finished paying off a gambling debt to one friend, he was taking a new loan from somebody else. At work, he tried to figure out how he could steal money from the cash register drawer without getting caught.*

Anorexia/Bulimia and Compulsive Overeating

Patrice had begun bingeing on food (eating a large quantity of food in a short period of time) and then purging (eliminating the food, either by vomiting or using laxatives). Or she would follow a binge with sessions of intense exercise in an attempt to work off the calories she just consumed.

Patrice started this behavior after her girlfriends had told her she was getting fat—although in fact she had just experienced a typical thirteen-year-old's growth spurt. Patrice also went through periods of anorexia, when she would eat only tiny amounts. After an anorexic period, she would always go back to bingeing.

As her eating disorder worsened, Patrice became secretive about her eating. She sneaked food from the kitchen and took it to her bedroom to binge on. To hide her purging, she ran the water in the bathroom sink to drown out the sound of her vomiting.

For someone with an eating disorder, even regular mealtimes
can cause fear and anxiety.

26 *Patrice's twin obsessions—food and being thin—ruled her life. Her head was usually full of thoughts about how many calories she had eaten and how many hours of exercise it would take to burn them off—but also of what other tempting leftovers were still available in the family refrigerator.*

Drug Abuse

Jennifer had always felt like a lost soul. She lived with her mother and her older brother, who were hardly ever home. When her mother did spend time at home, it was often with her boyfriend of the moment. She paid little attention to Jennifer.

School was no better. The girls at school were unfriendly, and Jennifer kept to herself in order to avoid being teased. As for boys, Jennifer felt totally incapable of talking to them.

Jennifer's brother had introduced her to pot when she was twelve. She had immediately liked the way it made her feel—happy and at peace. She no longer felt lonely. She couldn't wait to try it again.

Jennifer soon got to know the kids at school who smoked pot. She quickly became a regular user. The drug made both school and the lonely hours at home bearable. Also, pot was easier to get than alcohol.

By the time she was fourteen, Jennifer had | **27**
been introduced to speed and cocaine. She
especially liked speed, which made her feel
beautiful and sophisticated. But it quickly
seemed that she needed more and more of it
to get the high she wanted—and it was
expensive. Jennifer began to steal from her
mother's purse and to shoplift.

It wasn't long before Jennifer was caught
shoplifting at a local store. When her mother
learned that her daughter had been stealing
to get drugs, she was furious. The relationship
between mother and daughter had already
been bad. Now it became intolerable.

At sixteen, Jennifer moved in with an older
boy, Carl, who had been selling her drugs. She
became his live-in girlfriend in exchange for the
drugs she so badly needed. She wasn't in love
with Carl. In fact, they seldom talked. Jennifer
didn't care. At least, with this arrangement, she
got her drugs free.

Codependency

Maria is not a compulsive eater, an alcoholic, a
drug abuser, or a compulsive gambler. Yet she
has a very serious obsessive-compulsive
problem: codependency. She can't stop trying to
control the behavior of her boyfriend Carlos.

A codependent relationship is one in which
one person is obsessed with the other person

If you suffer from codependency, you spend time fulfilling other people's needs instead of taking care of your own.

in the relationship, and is driven to try to control his or her feelings and actions.

Maria is obsessed with the fear that Carlos may become angry with her and tell her he doesn't love her anymore. He tends to be moody and has already blown up at Maria a number of times.

Maria's thoughts are always on Carlos—trying to figure out what kind of mood he is in and, if his mood seems to be worsening, on how to avoid getting yelled at. When Carlos seems angry or upset, Maria is so distracted she can't concentrate in school.

Maria has been told many times that she worries too much about Carlos. Her friends are concerned that she should focus more on the rest of her life. Maria has tried, but she just can't seem to do it.

Although Maria knows that certain things provoke Carlos—like asking him to stop smoking or reminding him about his home-work assignments—she can't seem to keep from doing them. And she can't seem to stop overapologizing when Carlos gets mad at her—whether or not she has done anything wrong.

Although Maria has been told many times that she should break up with Carlos, she can't. She doesn't know what she would do without him.

30   You have just read descriptions of people who could be helped by a Twelve Step Program. Do any of them remind you of yourself? The descriptions are a good starting point to help you determine whether you have a problem.

Even this collection of stories does not represent the full variety of people who have obsessive-compulsive problems. Many people, for example, have more than one compulsion. They may be both bulimic and alcoholic, or abuse both drugs and alcohol.

Do You Have a Problem?

There are a few key questions you can ask yourself if you're struggling with identifying a problem.

These questions can be applied to many obsessive-compulsive problems. But you can also find others. See the Where to Go for Help section at the end of this book for more information on resources that can help you.

1. Have you ever decided to stop drinking, bingeing, taking drugs, or gambling for good—or even for a week—but lasted for only a couple of days?

How can you tell when you have a problem?

2. Do you wish people would stop telling you what to do?

3. Do you make excuses for your behavior or someone else's?

4. Have you been getting into trouble at home or at school?

5. Do you envy people who can drink, eat, take drugs, or gamble without getting into trouble?

6. Do you tell yourself you can stop any time you want to, even though you keep on drinking or taking drugs,

bingeing, gambling, or controlling someone else when you don't mean to?

7. Have you missed days of school or work because you were drunk or high, bingeing, or betting on a game? Or did you miss because someone else said he or she needed you?

8. Have you ever felt that your life would be better if you didn't drink or take drugs, binge, gamble, or become so wrapped up in your relationship with your boyfriend or girlfriend?

If you answered yes to three or more of these questions, you may have an obsessive-compulsive problem.

If you think you may have a problem, it's important to reach out for help. Find an adult you can trust—your parents or a friend's parents, a teacher, counselor, or coach. Even if you don't know the person very well, he or she can still listen to you and talk with you about what to do.

Only you can decide what kind of help is right for you. But learning more about the Twelve Steps—which comes in the next chapter—may help you to choose a path to successful, permanent recovery.

CHAPTER 3

How Do the Twelve Steps Work?

*H*ow do the Twelve Steps Work? They work when you work them.

This may sound like a clever but meaningless expression. But it isn't. Recovery by means of the Steps requires lots of hard work—a 100 percent effort, in fact. Working the Steps may well be the hardest thing a person ever does in his or her life.

The process is difficult, but it isn't impossible. Nor is it complicated. The Twelve Steps have made possible the recovery of thousands of alcoholics, compulsive gamblers, compulsive eaters, and others.

Following is a brief explanation of the Steps, how they work, and how to work them.

Successfully going through the Twelve Step Program brings freedom from obsessive-compulsive behavior.

1. We admitted that we were powerless over alcohol—that our lives had become unmanageable.

The First Step is the one step that can't be "worked." But that doesn't mean that Step One isn't important, or that it can be skipped over. Instead, this step is what makes all the following steps possible.

In order to take the First Step, you must have an experience called a "bottom." This is a feeling of total and utter despair upon glimpsing the truth of your situation.

People with obsessive-compulsive problems, such as alcoholics and drug addicts, compulsive eaters, and compulsive gamblers, may spend many years denying that they are in trouble. They seem unable to admit, or even see, that their illness has had devastating effects and that they have been powerless to change its downward progression.

For example, alcoholics tell themselves that they don't have a problem because they still have their job, they don't drink before noon, or they haven't yet been arrested on a DWI (driving while intoxicated) charge. Compulsive eaters deny that they are hurting themselves physically and emotionally by overeating.

But at "bottom," the denial syndrome breaks down. The alcoholic can admit that even though he hasn't been arrested on a DWI charge, or hasn't lost his job, it is only a matter of time before he has. The compulsive eater can admit that she is unable to stop compulsively overeating.

In this "moment of truth," a person is able to see and admit how out of control his or her life is, no matter what it may look like on the surface. These admissions of truth are painful, but they are essential before you can proceed with the rest of the Steps.

2. Came to believe that a Power greater than ourselves could restore us to sanity.

In Step Two you must get to the point where you can honestly say that you believe there is some kind of higher power that is interested in you and is capable of helping you turn your life around.

You don't need to be a practicing member of any established religion (or even believe in God) in order to get started on the Twelve Step Program. You only have to be open-minded about the existence of a God. It isn't necessary to adopt any particular conception of God, just one that makes sense for you.

For people who are struggling with this step, the chapter in the Big Book called "To Agnostics" is often helpful.

3. Made a decision to turn our will and our lives over to the care of God <u>as we understood Him</u>.

With Step Three, you actually enter into a relationship with the God you came to believe in from the previous step. You make a decision to live your life, from this point forward, as you think God would have you.

The choice to live in harmony with God's will rather than on the basis of self-will is no light decision. It's especially hard for people with an obsessive-compulsive problem, because the problem isolates them from others and often causes them to disregard other people's feelings.

Also, when you make the Third Step decision, it's a decision for a lifetime. You can't do it on a trial basis—"I'll live this way for a while and see what happens."

Because it is such an important step, the Third Step decision isn't made only in the quiet of your own thoughts. It must be voiced aloud and, if at all possible, in the

38 presence of another person who understands what you are trying to do. Suggestions for what to say when you make your Third Step commitment are provided in the Big Book.

Many people experience dramatic results after taking the Third Step. Often, they feel that their alcohol, drug, or compulsive eating problem has been removed.

Many people also experience a new sense of well-being and peace, and a belief that they can handle things. The future begins to look bright and hopeful rather than bleak.

4. Made a searching and fearless moral inventory of ourselves.

Step Four is a pen-and-paper step. To complete it, you need to make several lists. These lists will help you identify and face the specific acts and patterns that have been self-destructive.

In one list, you write down your various "character defects"—flaws such as "cheating," "stealing," "laziness," "blaming others." In others, you list and analyze all your resentments and fears. In still another, you analyze the relationships you have had, and develop an ideal for your behavior in future relationships.

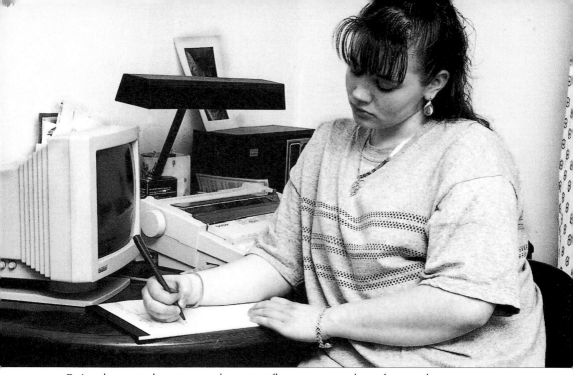

Being honest about your character flaws can produce fear and anxiety, but it is an essential step toward recovery.

Thoroughness and honesty are critical to completing this step successfully. By the time you reach the end you should have squarely faced some pretty uncomfortable truths about yourself and should be beginning to want to set right your past mistakes.

5. Admitted to God, to ourselves, and to another human being the exact nature of our wrongs.

It's easy to minimize the harm you have done, or to skip over some problems altogether when working on a personal inventory (the process described in the Fourth Step) all by yourself. The next step in the "cleaning out" process you begin in Step

40 Four requires that you read the lists that you made in the Fourth Step to another person. By admitting to another person the specifics of where and how you have gone wrong, you are better able to admit these things fully to God and yourself.

The Big Book gives valuable guidance on selecting an appropriate person to hear a Fourth Step inventory.

By the end of the Fifth Step, many people experience a keen sense of God's presence and an awareness that their drinking, drug use, eating, or other problem has truly been lifted from them.

6. Were entirely ready to have God remove all these defects of character.

It is one thing to admit to a problem and quite another to be truly willing to solve the problem. At Step Six, you must become honest with yourself as to whether you really are ready to have your defects removed. If not, you ask God to give you the willingness.

7. Humbly asked God to remove our shortcomings.

When you are entirely ready to be rid of all your resentments, fears, and defects, you ask God to take them from you.

Many people can relate dramatic stories of longtime fears and resentments being lifted from them when they take this step.

8. Made a list of all persons we had harmed, and became willing to make amends to them all.

9. Made direct amends to such people wherever possible, except when to do so would injure them or others.

These two steps are critical to moving successfully toward full recovery.

Making amends takes time and effort, careful thought, and often money. But it is essential to make up for all the harm that an obsessive-compulsive illness has caused.

If you have been disrespectful and unloving toward your parents, you must go out of your way to spend time with them and to show appreciation for all they have done for you. If you have shoplifted or stolen, you must replace or pay for what you have taken.

Some situations are delicate, such as those involving family, close friends, or old boyfriends or girlfriends, all of whom could be hurt easily. In such cases it is a

It's important to make amends for the harm you may have caused others. Sometimes, a sincere apology is all that's necessary.

good idea to consult with someone more experienced in recovery about the best way to make amends.

Most people experience a tremendous sense of release and freedom before they have even finished with the amends process. They become aware that they are able to perceive things and to do things they never could before.

10. Continued to take personal inventory and when we were wrong promptly admitted it.

While steps One through Nine are each done only once, step Ten is the first of three maintenance steps. This means that, once you are fairly well along in the amends process, **43** these steps should be done every day in order to maintain your recovery.

Step Ten is a shorter version of Steps Four through Nine. It requires you to keep a close watch on yourself throughout the day, identifying and admitting resentments, lies, fears, and selfish behavior, and promptly making amends for whatever you have done wrong.

11. **Sought through prayer and meditation to improve our conscious contact with God <u>as we understood Him</u>, praying only for knowledge of His will for us and the power to carry that out.**

The Big Book gives helpful suggestions for prayer and meditation, but it also recommends that people consult their priest, minister, or rabbi or any of the many helpful books available on these subjects.

Many people find, as they progress in recovery, that they don't always need to say a formal prayer in order to receive guidance. They develop a kind of "sixth sense" about what to do in difficult situations or about courses of action they should pursue or avoid.

Meditation and prayer are a beneficial part of a Twelve Step Program.

12. Having had a spiritual awakening as the result of these steps, we tried to carry this message to alcoholics, and to practice these principles in all our affairs.

In order to maintain recovery, it is essential that you share what you have found with others who still suffer from alcoholism or other kinds of obsessive-compulsive problems.

The Big Book provides extensive guidance on how to identify people who are likely candidates for recovery and then on how to help them through the Steps.

Getting Started

If you still don't feel confident enough to

set out on your own to work the Steps, you aren't alone. That is why Twelve Step fellowships exist.

Meetings of such fellowships as Alcoholics Anonymous, Al-Anon, Narcotics Anonymous, Overeaters Anonymous, and Gamblers Anonymous provide places to get help in working the Program. These fellowships hold regular meetings in thousands of cities all over the world.

Usually these organizations have a listing in the local telephone directory. You can call and talk to someone about the Program, or find out times and locations of meetings in the area.

Meetings of anonymous fellowships may have a variety of formats. Some feature a speaker who talks about his or her experiences in the illness and in recovery. Others are devoted to studying the Twelve Steps or the Big Book in depth.

Most meetings, whatever their format, include a period during which anyone who wants to is invited to "share," or speak. People may discuss problems they are having, report on progress they have made, ask a question, or simply comment on something said earlier in the meeting.

Anyone with an honest interest in recovery can attend most meetings. But you

Twelve Step fellowships exist in thousands of cities all around the world. You can find a local meeting in the telephone book.

may want to ask whether a particular meeting is nonsmoking, "men only" or "women only," or closed to people who do not have the particular problem addressed by that fellowship.

Sponsors

A meeting is also a place where someone interested in recovery can find a sponsor. A sponsor is a person who has already been through the Twelve Steps and is qualified to guide a newcomer.

Although it is possible to work the Steps on your own with just the Big Book as a guide, the vast majority of people find it tremendously helpful to work with a sponsor.

Most people talk to their sponsors every day, or at least several times a week. Sponsors help them be honest with themselves about what is going on in their lives. This is always a big task for a recovering person. Sponsors also provide advice and guidance about working the Program.

A good way to find a sponsor is to go to a few meetings and listen to various people share. If someone sounds as if he or she "has something you want," you should consider him or her a strong candidate.

It is also a good idea, before agreeing to work with a person, to make sure the information he or she gives you corresponds

A sponsor is a person who has already been through the Twelve Steps and is thereby qualified to guide a newcomer through them.

with that in the Big Book. This way, you can make sure the guidance the person gives you will be in line with the way the Program is supposed to be worked.

Unfortunately, people sometimes advertise themselves as sponsors who may not have actually worked the Steps. They may mean well, but they are not yet qualified to guide someone else through them. Choose a sponsor with care!

You Aren't Alone

If what you have read in this chapter sounds a little intimidating, don't worry. You aren't alone! Many people, both young and old, are reluctant to go to a meeting where they may

not know anybody. They may be even more
reluctant to talk about their personal lives in
front of a group of strangers.

Others fear they will never will be able to
do some of the things the Steps require, such
as coming clean with their parents, paying
back money they owe, or reading their
Fourth Step inventory to another person.

Still others even worry that if they live the
kind of life they think God would like them
to live, they will become dull and boring
people. They fear their friends will drop them.

These are all very common fears—and
fears that people master every day.

*Karen knew she had an eating disorder that
was steadily getting worse. But she put off
going to a meeting of Overeaters Anonymous
for a long time.*

*Karen prided herself on her sophistication.
From what she had heard of them, she
thought Twelve Step meetings were kind of
hokey and "not for her." She wasn't the kind
of person to spill her guts in front of a group.
She hadn't admitted to herself that she was
very much afraid of the exposure and honesty
involved in anonymous fellowship meetings.
Also, Karen was painfully shy.*

*Eventually, however, Karen's bulimia got
so bad that she could no longer concentrate*

50 *enough to go to classes. Desperation led her finally to call the O.A. number in the phone book. To her surprise, she found there was a meeting at a church right in her neighborhood, one she could even walk to. Getting herself to that first meeting was hard—but at least it was a little easier because it was in such a close and familiar place.*

Karen had never heard other people talk so openly about the same problem she had. She cried throughout that entire meeting. She was still too shy and fearful to speak to anyone, even though several people came up to her afterward and offered her their phone numbers in case she wanted to talk.

Karen went to the weekly meetings at the church for a month and a half, never opening her mouth. But she was still bingeing and purging. Finally, desperation again pushed her to take a step. She knew she needed a sponsor to help get her on a real path of recovery.

There was one woman, Maureen, who had impressed Karen the few times she had heard her speak. At the next meeting she asked Maureen to sponsor her. Maureen did not say yes immediately. Instead, she said she wanted to work with Karen for a week to determine whether she was a good candidate for recovery. Karen found this unnerving, but at the same time she was impressed. Clearly Maureen took the business of sponsorship very seriously.

At the end of the week, Karen was relieved to hear that Maureen believed she really did mean business about recovery and that Maureen would be her sponsor. Soon Karen was hard at work on the Steps. To her amazement, Karen found that the drive to binge and purge had been lifted.

Still, however, she felt totally unable to share at the meetings. At Maureen's suggestion, Karen was going to several meetings a week. But she was having problems with her boyfriend. He was glad her bulimia was under control, but wasn't happy about the time she spent at meetings. He wanted to know when she would be through with this "treatment" and able to spend more time with him again. Karen began to wonder whether recovery was worth it.

Then Karen took her Seventh Step. The night after she had humbly and sincerely asked God to remove her shortcomings, Karen attended her usual Friday night meeting. The session was a "topic" meeting—and the topic for that evening was "acquiring faith." Halfway through the sharing, Maureen looked Karen's way and announced, "I think Karen has something to say."

52 | *Karen suddenly found herself talking to the group about her own experiences. She couldn't believe she was actually speaking in front of all those people. Then she knew what it was—her Seventh Step had worked! She had overcome her shyness!*

From that night on, Karen was a regular contributor at meetings. Also from that time on, she stopped questioning her new way of life.

Eventually, Karen's boyfriend stopped calling her. But by the time Karen was finishing up her Ninth Step, it didn't matter too much anymore. She was excited about the new possibilities before her.

Karen had taken steps to mend her relationships with friends and family. She realized that when she was bingeing and purging, she had pushed them away—especially when they expressed concern for her. It wasn't long before Karen was meeting new people too.

It had been a long road, but Karen was glad to be living a healthy life again.

CHAPTER 4

How You Can Get Involved

What makes someone a good candidate for working the Twelve Steps successfully? A lot of it has to do with attitude. You have to be ready—really ready—to start recovery.

You can use this list to decide whether you are ready to work the Program.

1. You have reached a point of deep desperation.

2. You have enough self-honesty to admit the truth about your situation.

3. You want to quit for good.

4. You know you need help to quit.

What makes someone a good candidate for working the
Twelve Steps successfully? Attitude.

5. Your interest in recovery is sincere.

6. You want what you see and hear in
   other recovered people.

7. You are open-minded about the idea
   of God.

8. You are willing to do whatever it
   takes to work the Program.

If you think you might be a candidate for
working the Twelve Steps, you can contact
any of the anonymous fellowships men-
tioned in this book or listed in an appen-
dix in the back. Most have a listing in the
white pages of any local phone book.

If you are not sure which anonymous fellowship is right for you, don't despair. Compulsive eaters have found help at A.A. meetings, and alcoholics at meetings of Narcotics Anonymous. The most important thing is to find a group of people who have worked the Steps and who can help someone else work them. You will feel more comfortable after you attend a few meetings and see what it's all about.

Also, you may feel that the Twelve Steps aren't right for you. That's fine—they aren't for everyone! It's important to explore all your options before you decide which recovery route you think is best. There are other organizations, some of which are listed at the back of this book, that you can contact for help.

Just remember—full and permanent recovery *is* possible!

Glossary

anonymity   The state of being unnamed, unidentified.

anorexia   Eating disorder in which a person has an abnormal fear of gaining weight and thus resorts to starvation diets.

bulimia   Eating disorder in which a person eats voraciously, then resorts to vomiting or laxatives to remove the food.

codependency   Compulsion to enable another person to obtain his or her needs or wants to the exclusion of one's own.

compulsive   Relating to a psychological force that makes an action necessary.

denial   Defense mechanism in which a person is unable to admit a psychological problem such as alcoholism.

inventory Listing of personal attitudes and qualities or shortcomings.

isolation Deliberate setting apart of oneself or another person.

maintenance Continuation or perseverance in a course of action.

obsessive Characterized by an irresistible desire to perform an action.

rationalization Invention of untrue causes for an undesirable course of action.

recurring Tending to happen over and over again.

syndrome Group of signs or emotions that suggest a particular disorder.

Where to Go for Help

Twelve Step Fellowships

You can use these numbers in case there is no local number for the fellowship in your telephone book. Someone at a national office will be happy to tell you where the meeting nearest you can be found, as well as send you informational pamphlets.

Alcoholics Anonymous
(helps people with an alcohol problem)
A.A. World Services Inc.
P.O. Box 459
New York, NY 10163
(212) 870-3400
Web site: http:www.alcoholics-
   anonymous.org

Al-Anon Family Group Headquarters, Inc.
(helps people who have trouble living
   with an alcoholic or who have problems with codependency)

1600 Corporate Landing Parkway
Virginia Beach, VA 23456
(804) 563-1600
(800) 344-2666
Web site: http://www.al-anon.org/

Gamblers Anonymous
(helps people with a gambling problem)
P.O. Box 17173
Los Angeles, CA 90017
(213) 386-8789

Narcotics Anonymous
(helps people with narcotic addiction)
World Service Office
19737 Nordhoff Place
Chatsworth, CA 91311
(818) 773-9999
e-mail: wso@aol.com

Overeaters Anonymous
(helps people with problems with
compulsive eating, anorexia and bulimia)
World Service Office
6075 Zenith St. NE
Rio Rancho, NM 87124
(505) 891-4320
Web site: http://www.overeatersanony-
   mous.org/

60 | **The Recovery Alliance**
(helps people with any kind of
obsessive-compulsive problem)
P.O. Box 861
Milford, CT 06460
(203) 877-3336
Web site: http://www.recoveryalliance.org/

Other Sources for Help

**National Institute on Drug Abuse
(NIDA)**
Public Information Department
5600 Fishers lane, Room 1039A
Rockville, MD 20857
(800) 662-HELP
(301) 294-5401 fax
Web site: http://www.nida.nih.gov/
e-mail: information@www.nida.nih.gov

**You also can check this search, or
others like it, on the World Wide Web:**

http://www.yahoo.com/Health/Mental_
Health/Addiction_and_Recovery/
Twelve_Step_Approach

For Further Reading

Alcoholics Anonymous: The Story of How Many Thousands of Men and Women Have Recovered from Alcoholism. Alcoholics Anonymous World Services, Inc: 1986.

Glass, George. *Drugs and Fitting In.* New York: The Rosen Publishing Group, 1997.

Kolodny, Nancy. *When Food's a Foe: How to Confront and Conquer Your Eating Disorder.* Boston: Little, Brown, 1992.

Septien, Al. *Everything You Need to Know About Codependency.* New York: The Rosen Publishing Group. Rev. ed.1997.

Index

64 | *About the Author*

Susan Banfield is a freelance writer and editor whose work includes eight other young adult nonfiction titles and numerous newspaper and magazine articles. Ms. Banfield is also, thanks to the Twelve Steps, a recovered compulsive eater and anorexic/bulimic. Her career as a writer coincides with her years in recovery—both began fifteen years ago—and the first would not have been possible were it not for the second. Ms. Banfield lives in Milford, Connecticut.

Photo Credits

Cover by Les Mills; p. 25 by Bill Losh/FPG International; p. 28 by Ira Fox; p. 31 by Lauren Piperno; p. 42 by Kim Sonsky; p. 46 by John Novajosky; all other photos by Pablo Maldonado.